ULTIMATE GUITAR PLAY-ALONG

RADIOHEAD

Play Along with 8 Great-Sounding Tracks

BOOK & PLAY-ALONG CDS
WITH **TNT** TONE 'N' TEMPO CHANGER

T0040756

About the TNT Changer

Use the TNT software to change keys, loop playback, and mute tracks for play-along. For complete instructions, see the **TnT ReadMe.pdf** file on your enhanced CDs.

Windows users: insert a CD into your computer, double-click on My Computer, right-click on your CD drive icon, and select Explore to locate the file.

Mac users: insert a CD into your computer and double-click on the CD icon on your desktop to locate the file.

Produced by
Alfred Music Publishing Co., Inc.
P.O. Box 10003
Van Nuys, CA 91410-0003
alfred.com

Printed in USA.

ISBN-10: 0-7390-8655-3 (Book & 2 CDs)
ISBN-13: 978-0-7390-8655-1 (Book & 2 CDs)

Cover image from the original Faber Music cover by The Ghost & Stanley Donwood

 Alfred Cares. Contents printed on 100% recycled paper.

Contents

2+2=5

Words and Music by
THOMAS YORKE, JONATHAN GREENWOOD,
COLIN GREENWOOD, EDWARD O'BRIEN and PHILIP SELWAY

2+2=5 - 6 - 1

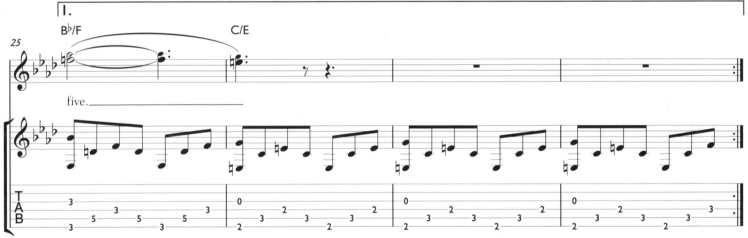

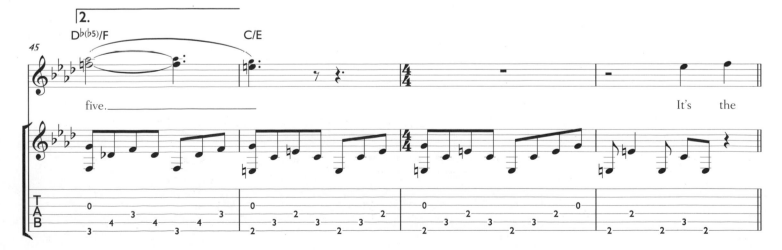

2+2=5 - 6 - 2

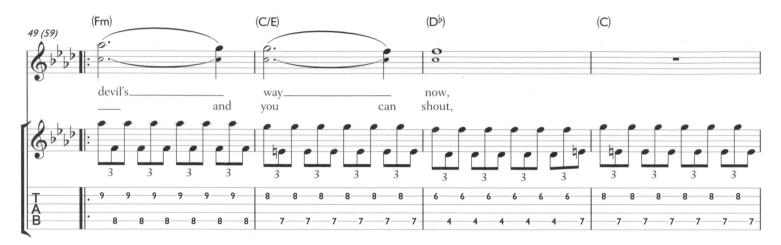

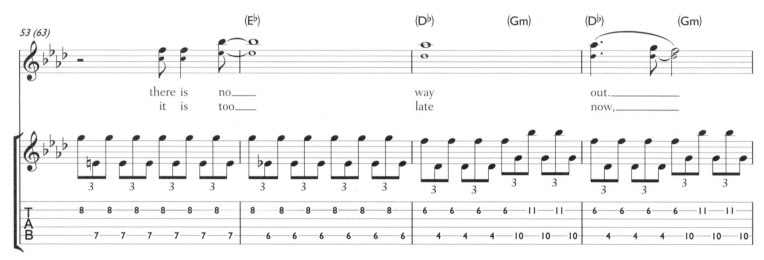

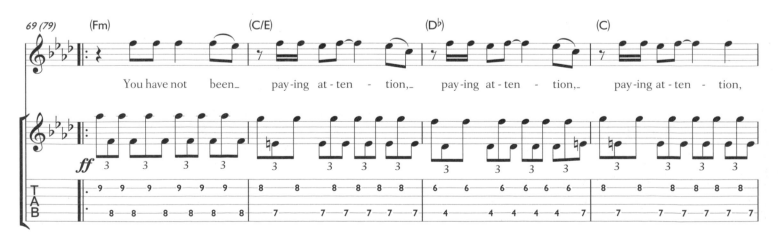

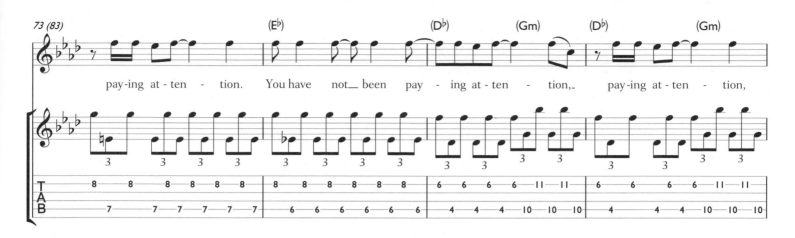

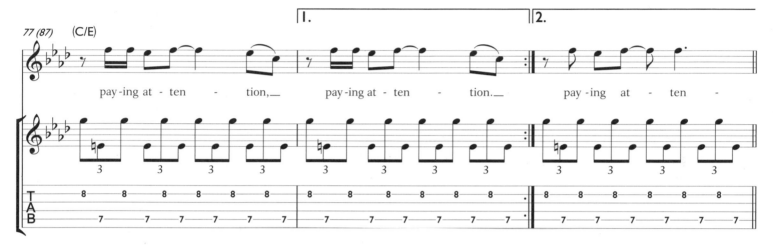

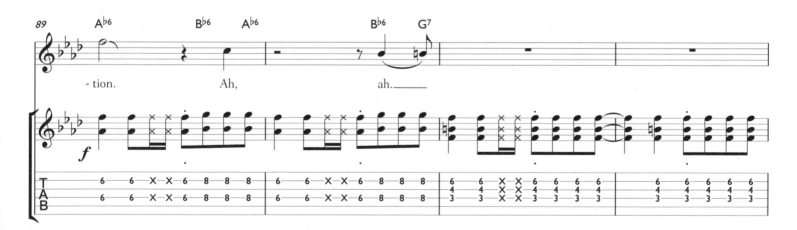

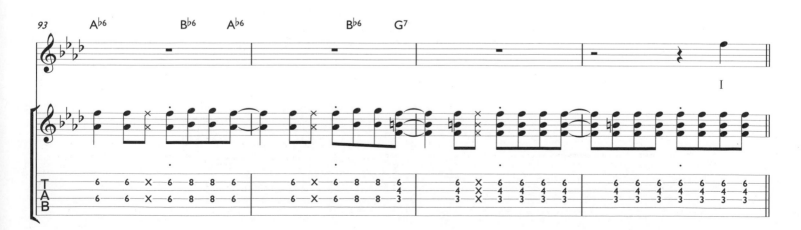

2+2=5 - 6 - 4

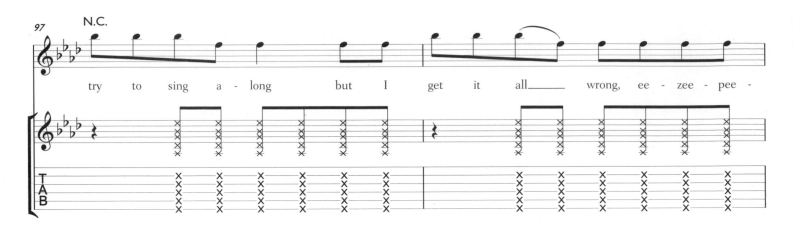

try to sing a - long but I get it all____ wrong, ee - zee - pee -

- zee, ee - zee - pee - zee. I

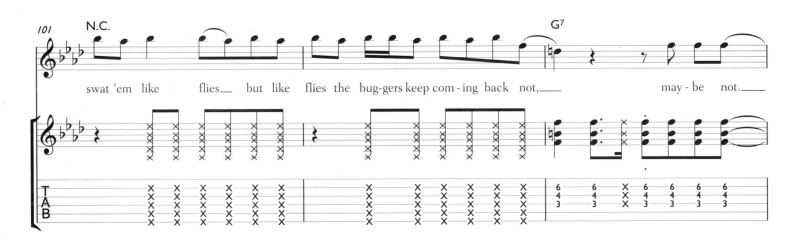

swat 'em like flies_ but like flies the bug-gers keep com-ing back not,___ may - be not.___

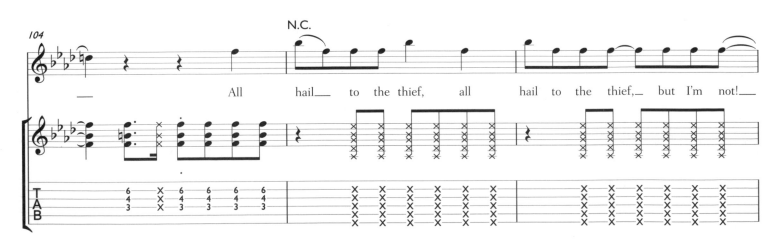

_ All hail_ to the thief, all hail to the thief,_ but I'm not!__

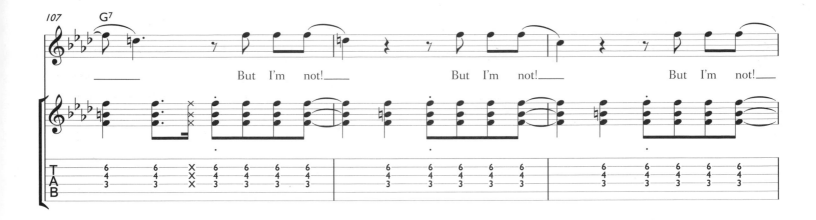

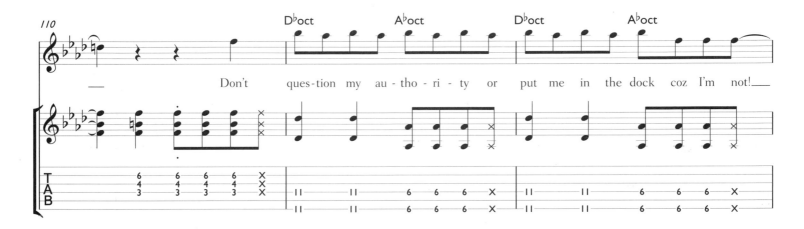

2+2=5 - 6 - 6

ANYONE CAN PLAY GUITAR

Words and Music by
THOMAS YORKE, JONATHAN GREENWOOD,
COLIN GREENWOOD, EDWARD O'BRIEN and PHILIP SELWAY

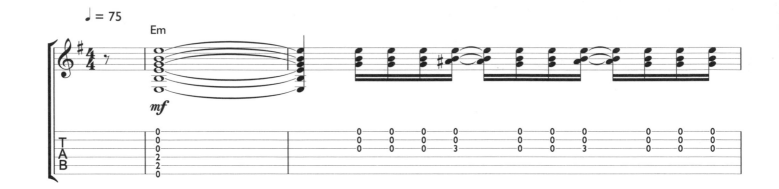

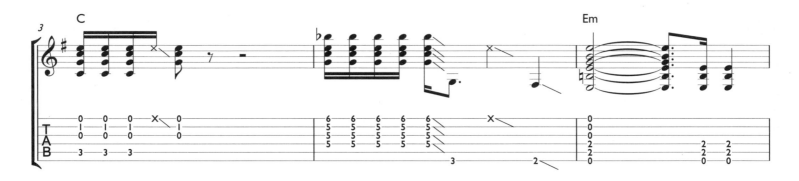

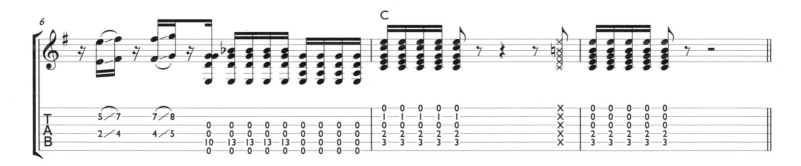

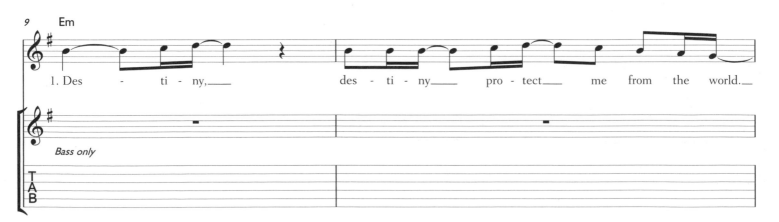

1. Des - ti - ny,___ des - ti - ny___ pro - tect___ me from the world.

Bass only

Anyone Can Play Guitar - 6 - 1

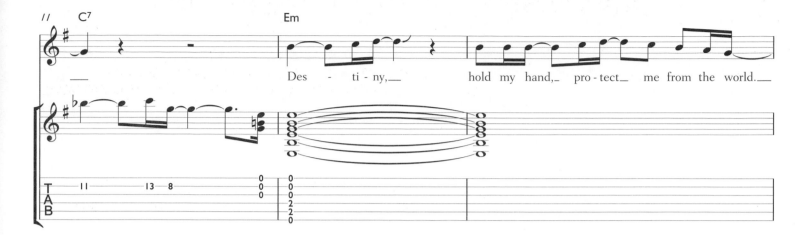

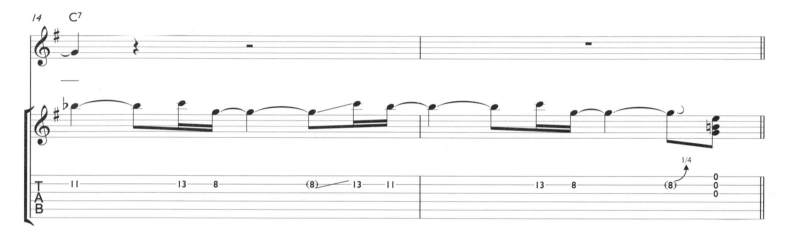

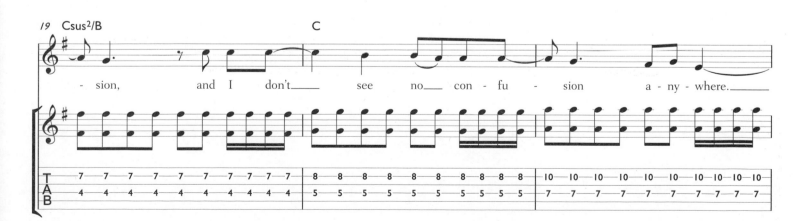

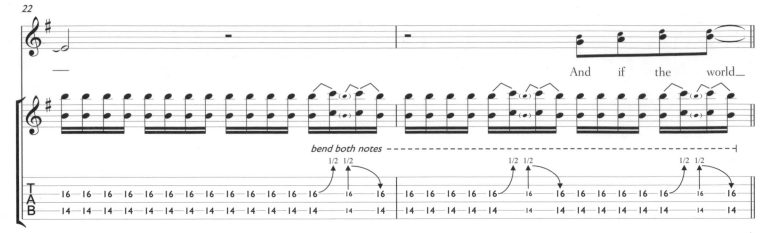

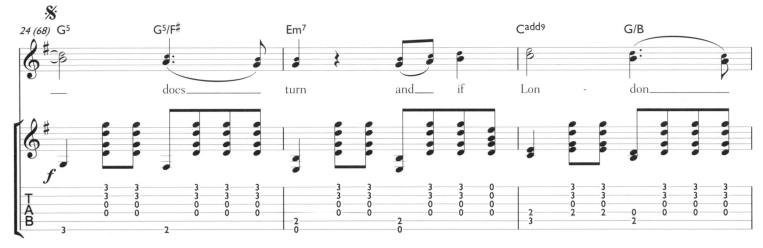

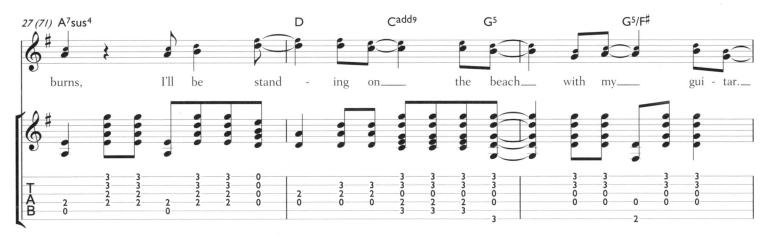

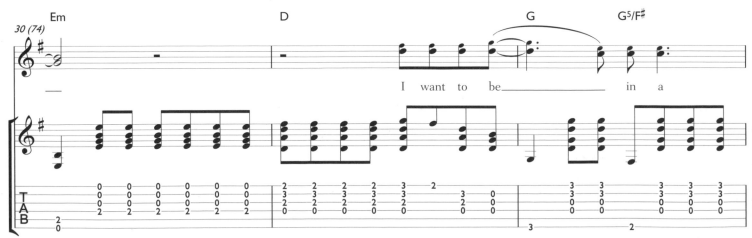

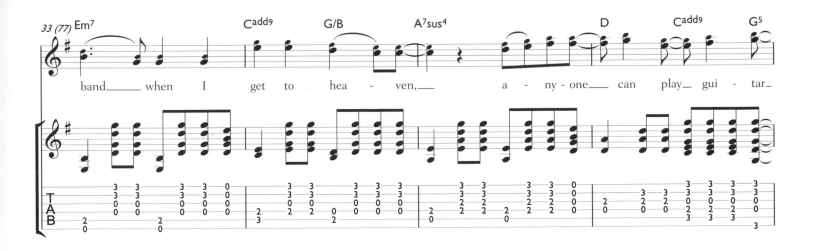

band___ when I get to hea - ven,___ a - ny-one___ can play___ gui - tar___

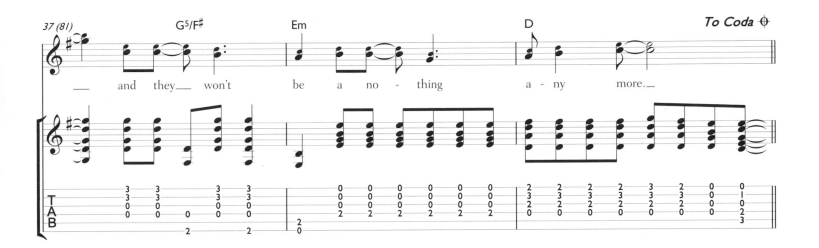

___ and they___ won't be a no - thing a - ny more.___

To Coda ⊕

tempo I (♩ = 75)

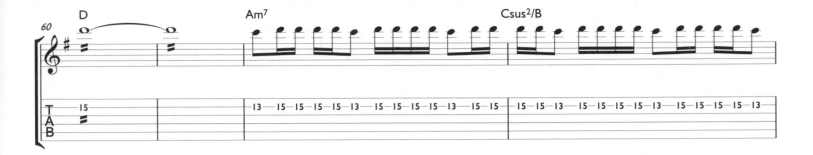

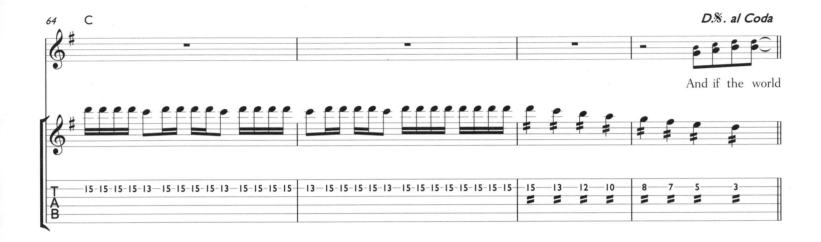

D.%. al Coda

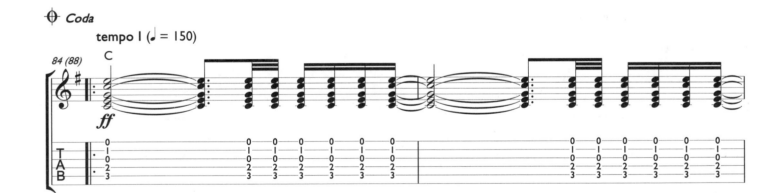

And if the world

Coda

tempo I (♩ = 150)

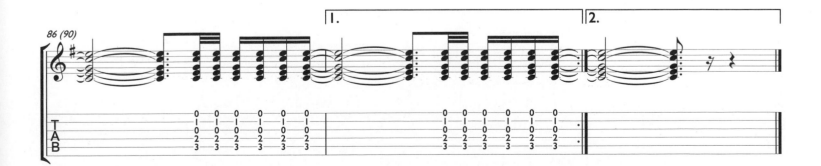

CREEP

Words and Music by
THOM YORKE, JONATHAN GREENWOOD,
PHILIP SELWAY, COLIN GREENWOOD, EDWARD O'BRIEN,
ALBERT HAMMOND and MIKE HAZELWOOD

Creep - 5 - 1

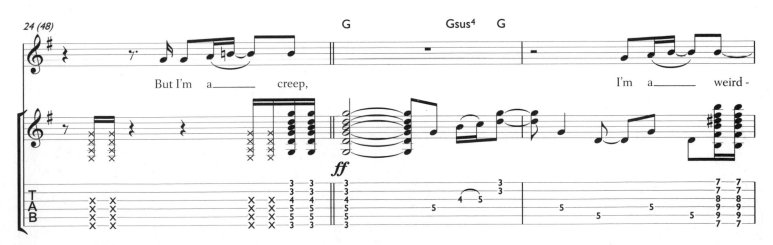

What the hell__ am I do-ing here?__

I don't be - long_____ here._____

2. I don't care if it hurts,__

_____ oh_____ She's run - ning out the door,__

she's_____ run - ning__ she

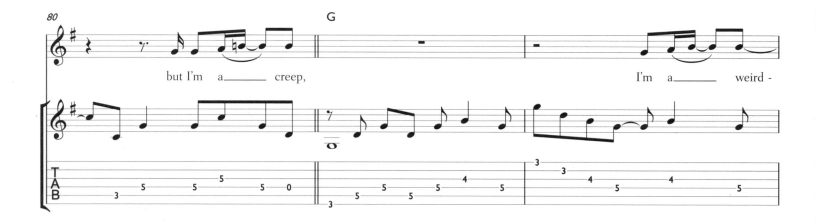

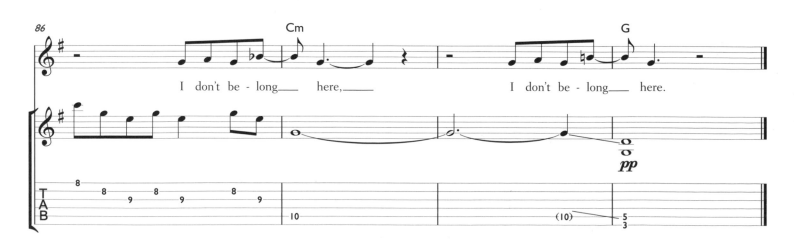

JUST

Words and Music by
THOMAS YORKE, JONATHAN GREENWOOD,
COLIN GREENWOOD, EDWARD O'BRIEN and PHILIP SELWAY

1. Can't get the stink off, he's been hang-ing round for days.
2. Don't get my sym-pa-thy, hang-ing out the fif-teenth

Just - 6 - 1

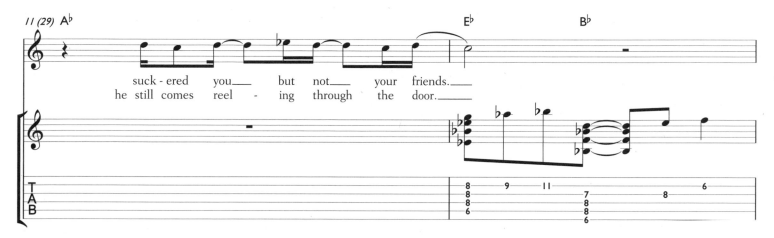

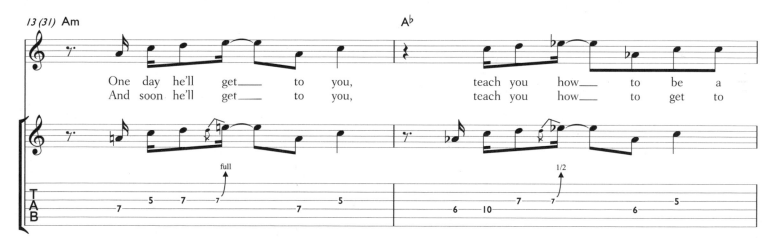

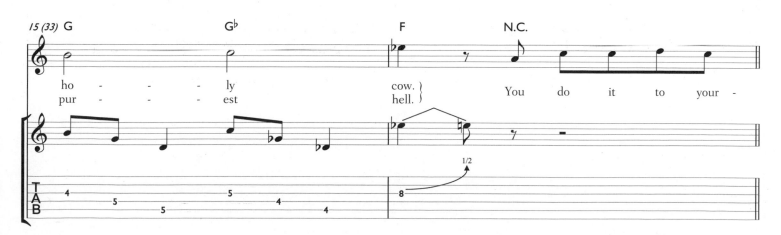

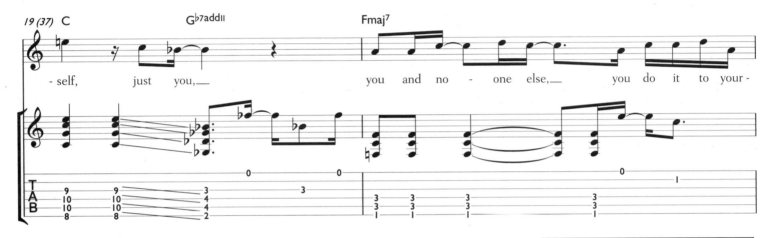

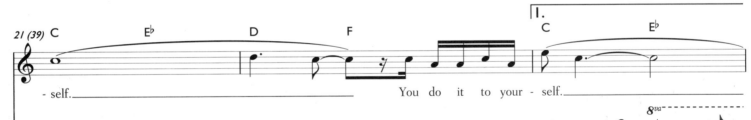

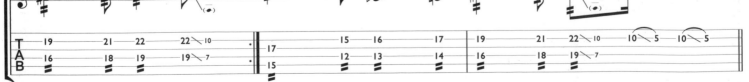

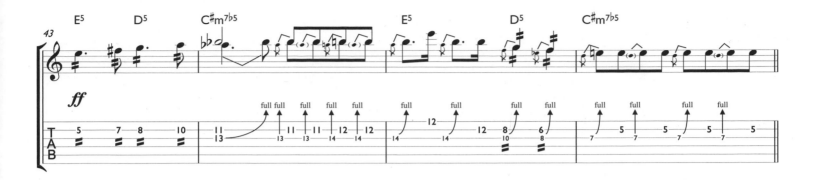

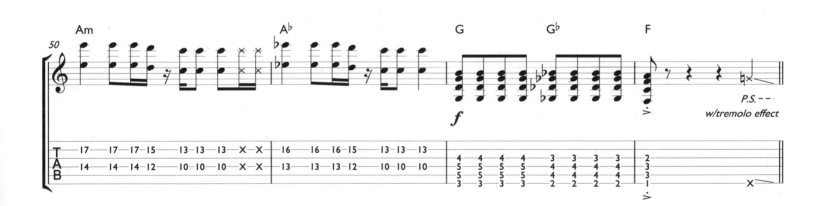

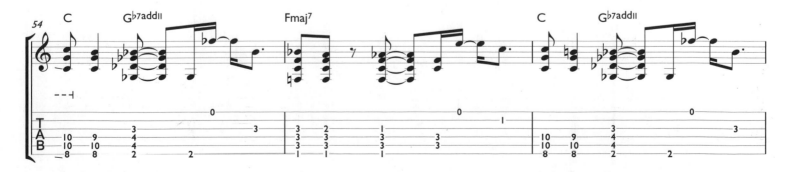

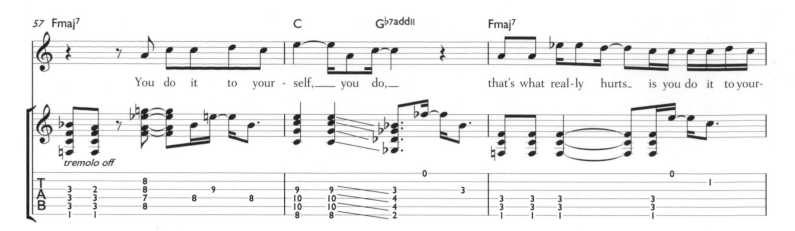

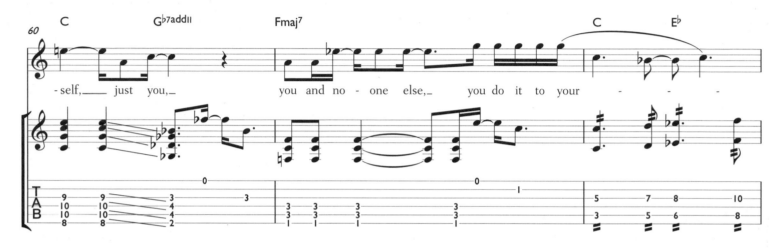

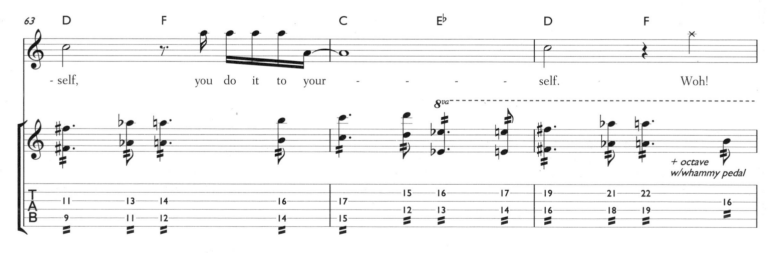

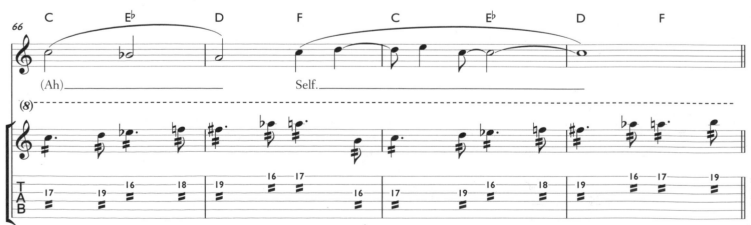

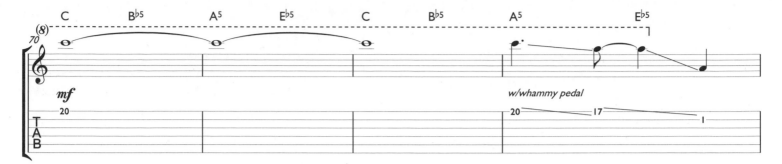

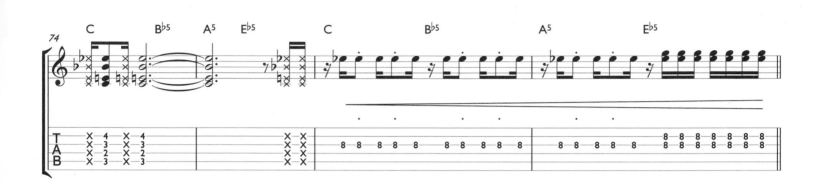

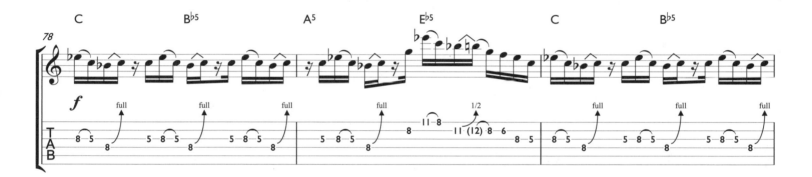

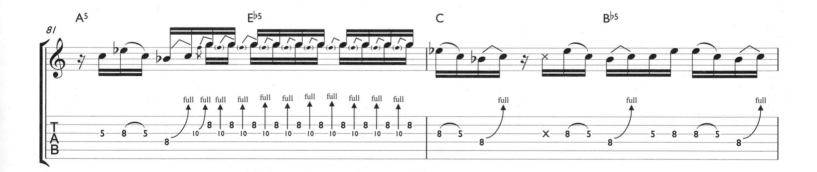

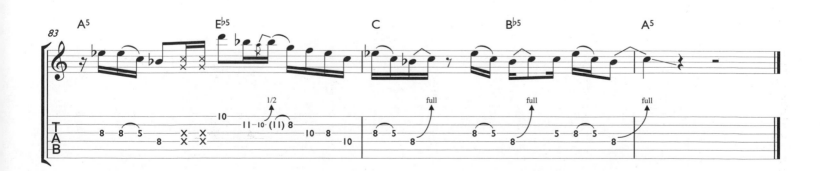

KNIVES OUT

Words and Music by
THOMAS YORKE, JONATHAN GREENWOOD,
COLIN GREENWOOD, EDWARD O'BRIEN and PHILIP SELWAY

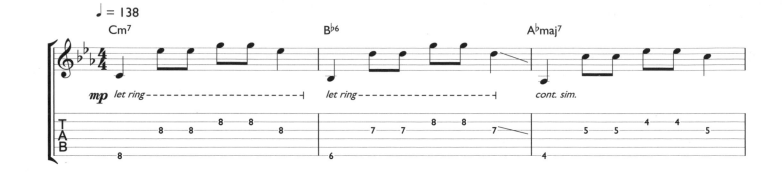

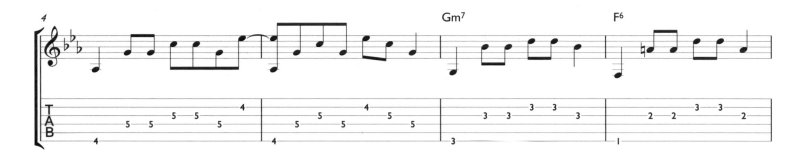

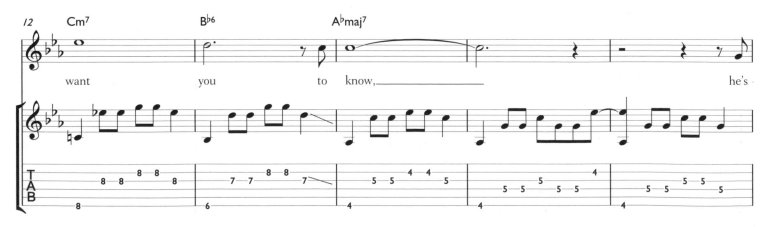

Knives Out - 8 - 1

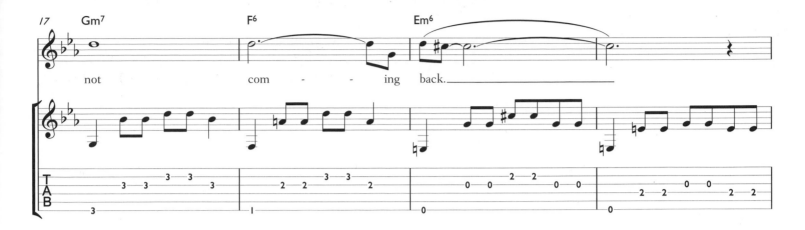

not com - - ing back._____

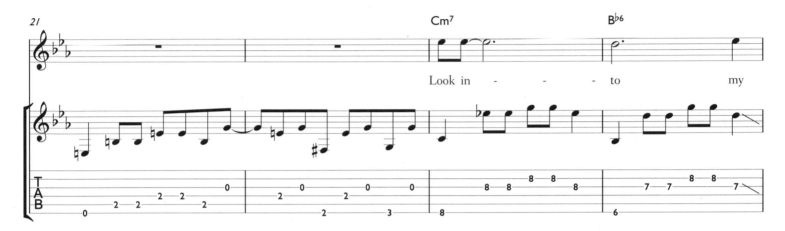

Look in - - to my

eyes,_____ I'm not com - ing

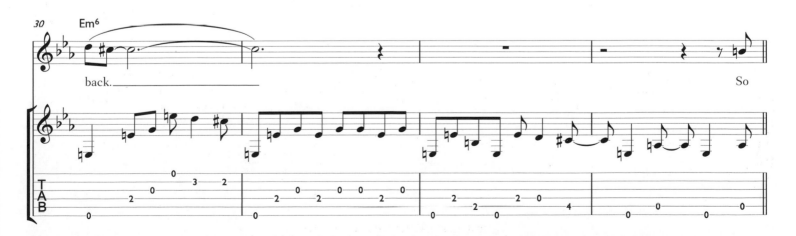

back._____ So

30

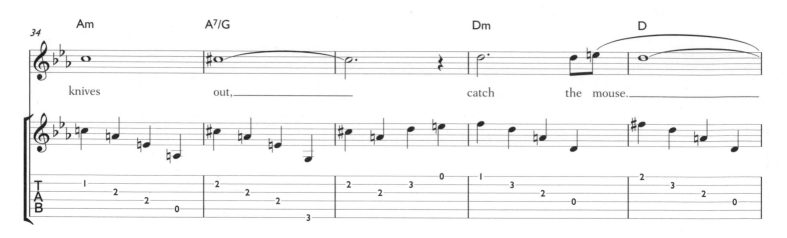

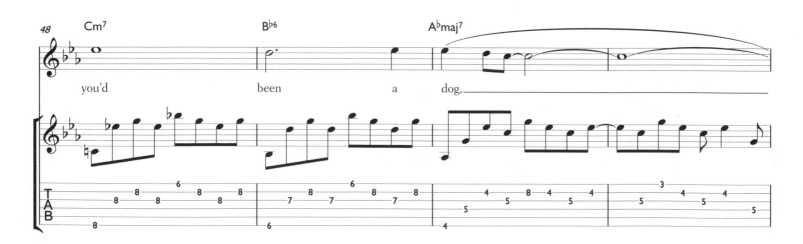

they would have drowned you_____ at birth._____

Look in ____

-to my eyes,_____ it's the

on - ly way you'll know I'm tell - ing the truth._____

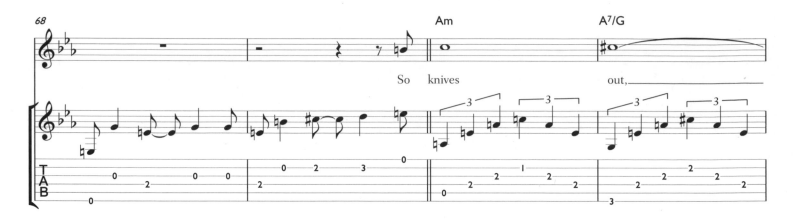

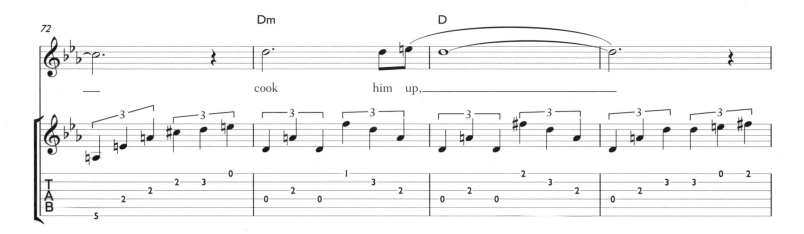

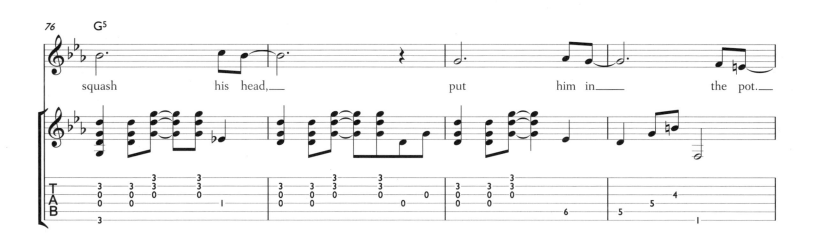

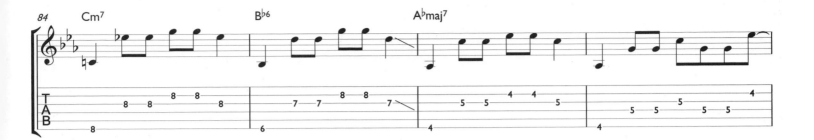

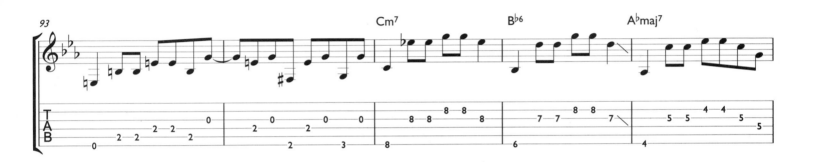

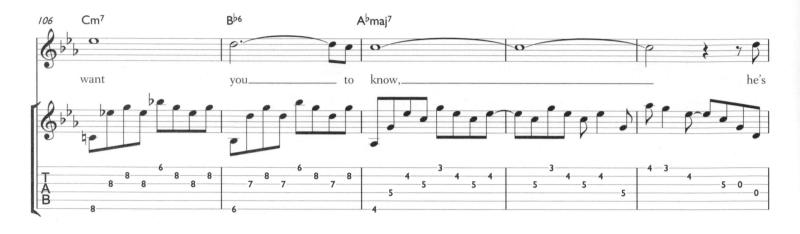

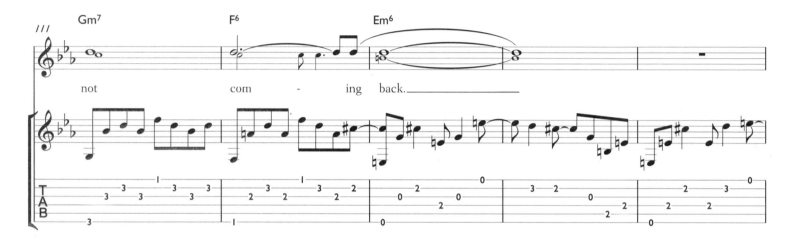

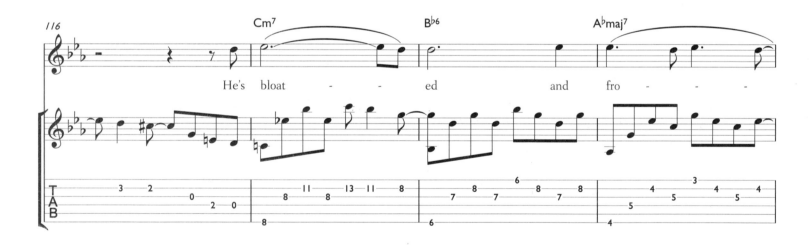

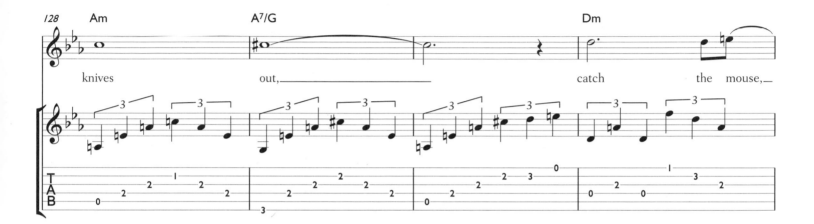

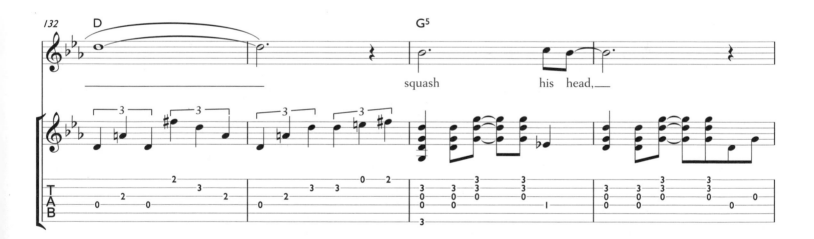

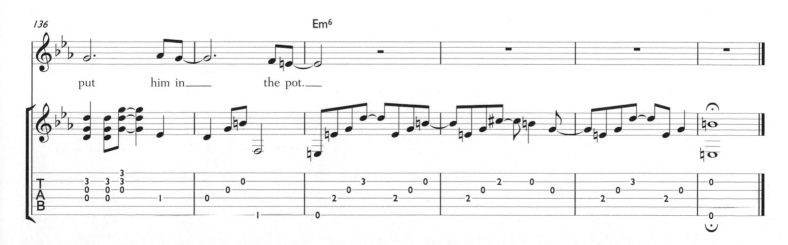

OPTIMISTIC

Words and Music by
THOMAS YORKE, JONATHAN GREENWOOD,
COLIN GREENWOOD, EDWARD O'BRIEN and PHILIP SELWAY

Optimistic - 9 - 1

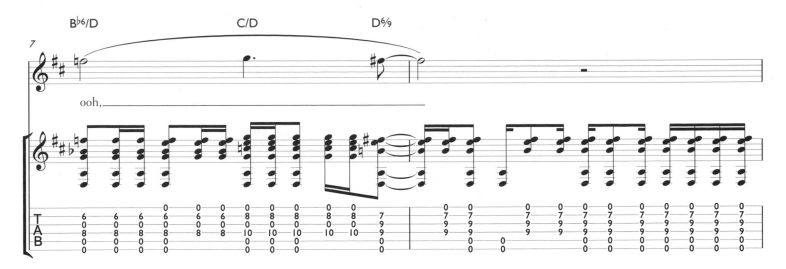

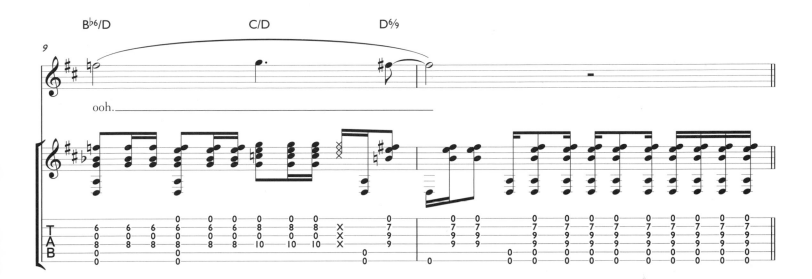

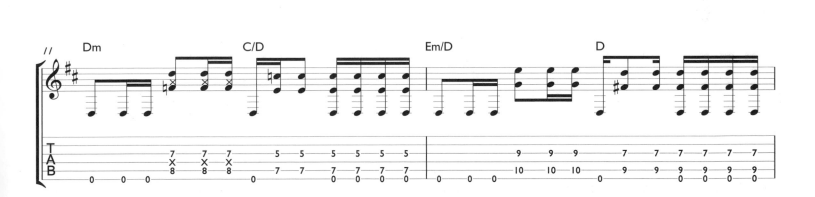

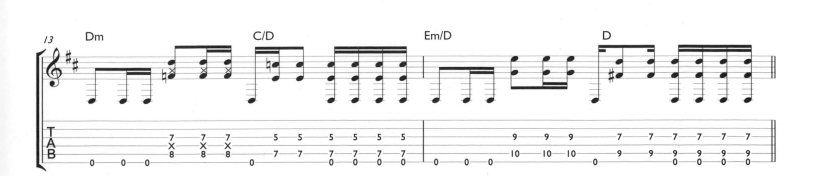

Optimistic - 9 - 2

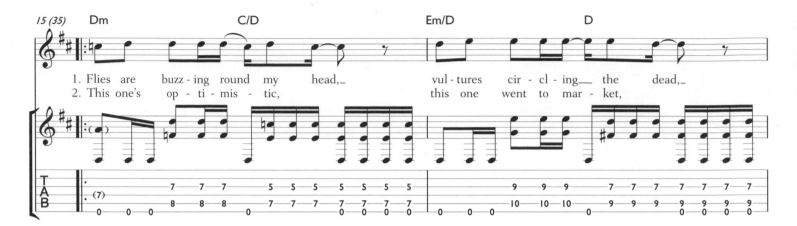

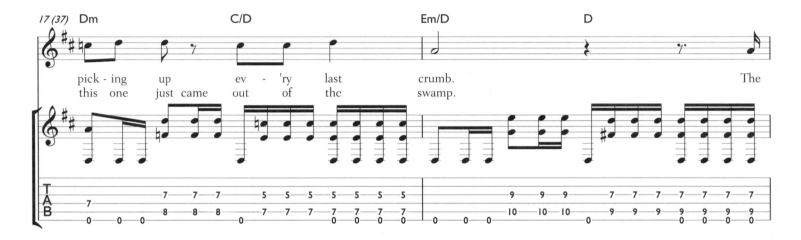

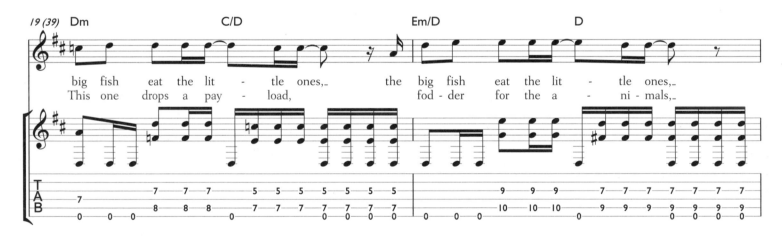

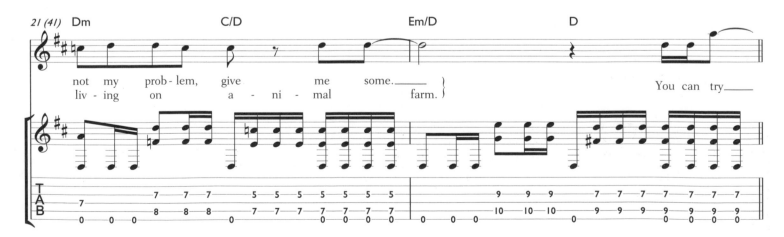

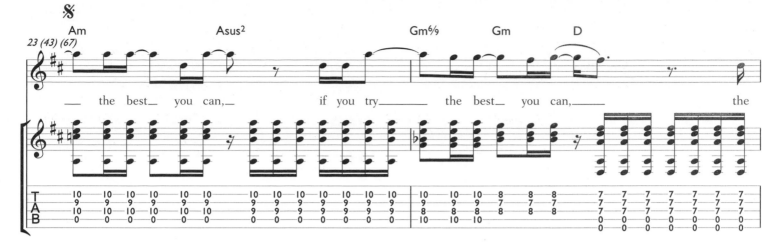

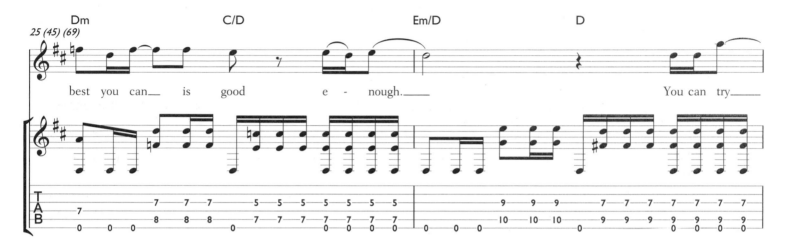

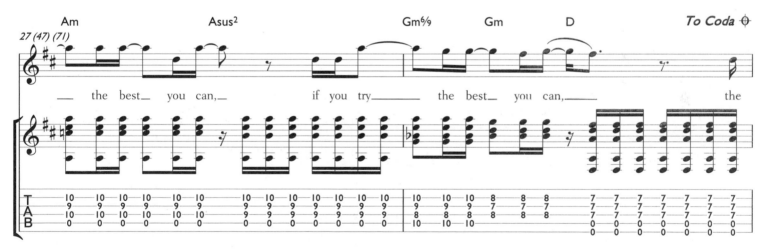

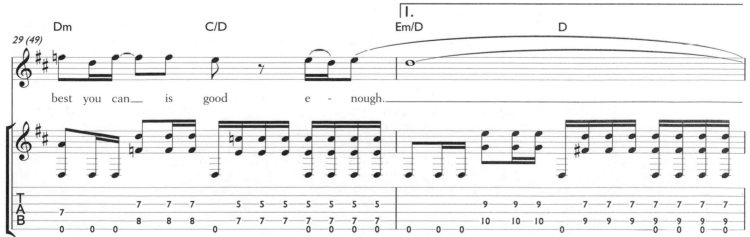

Optimistic - 9 - 4

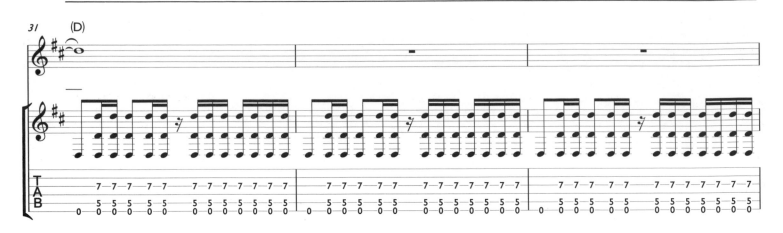

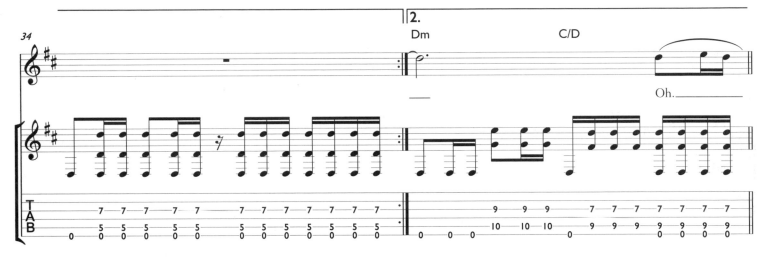

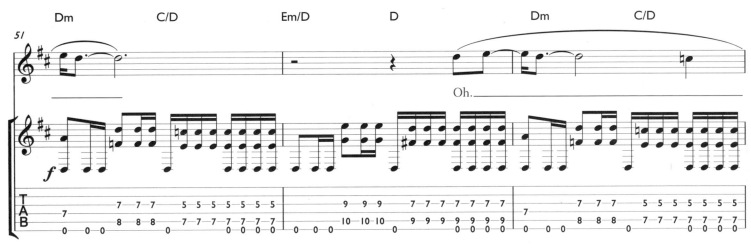

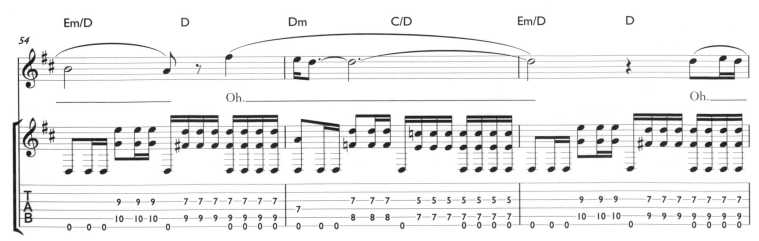

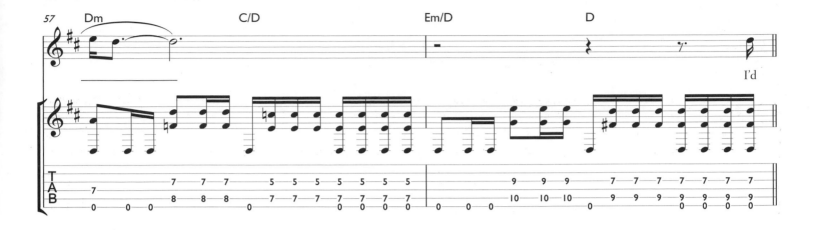

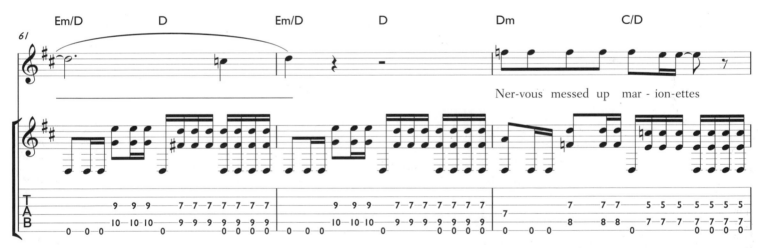

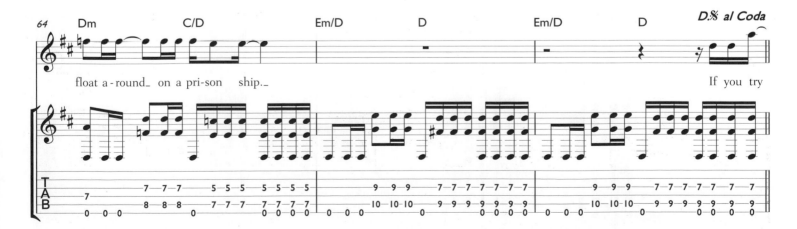

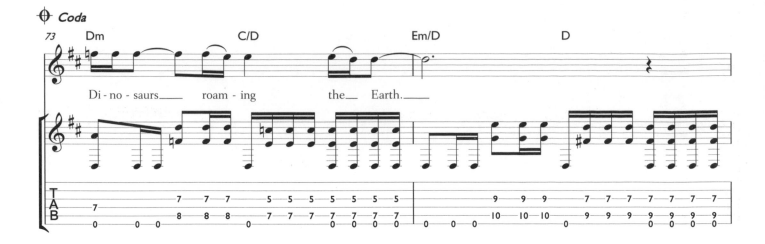

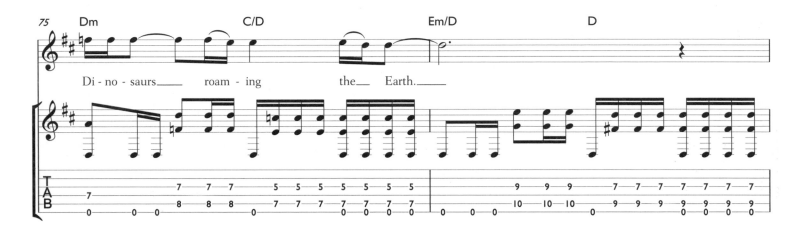

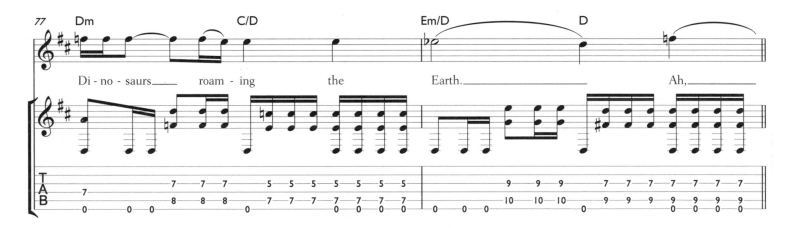

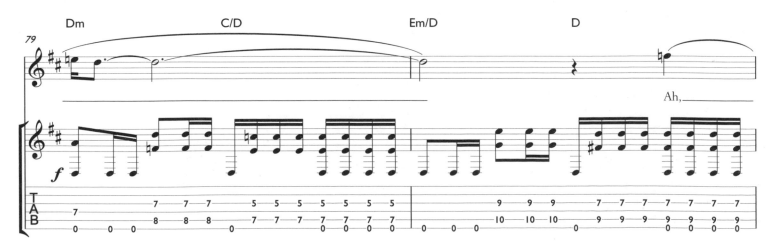

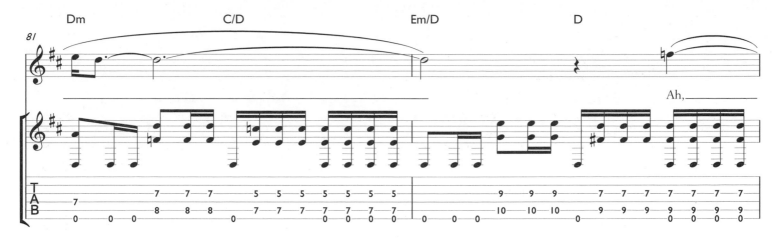

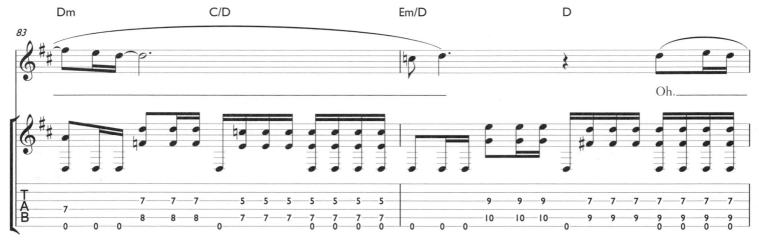

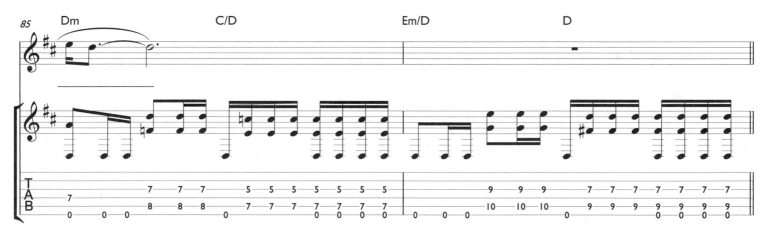

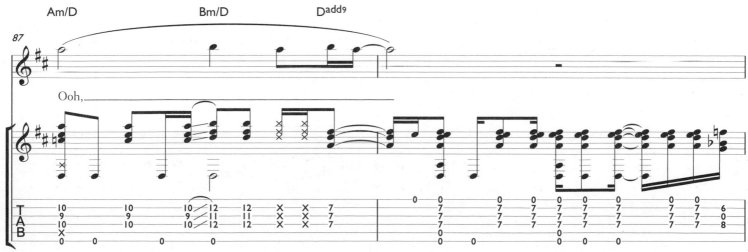

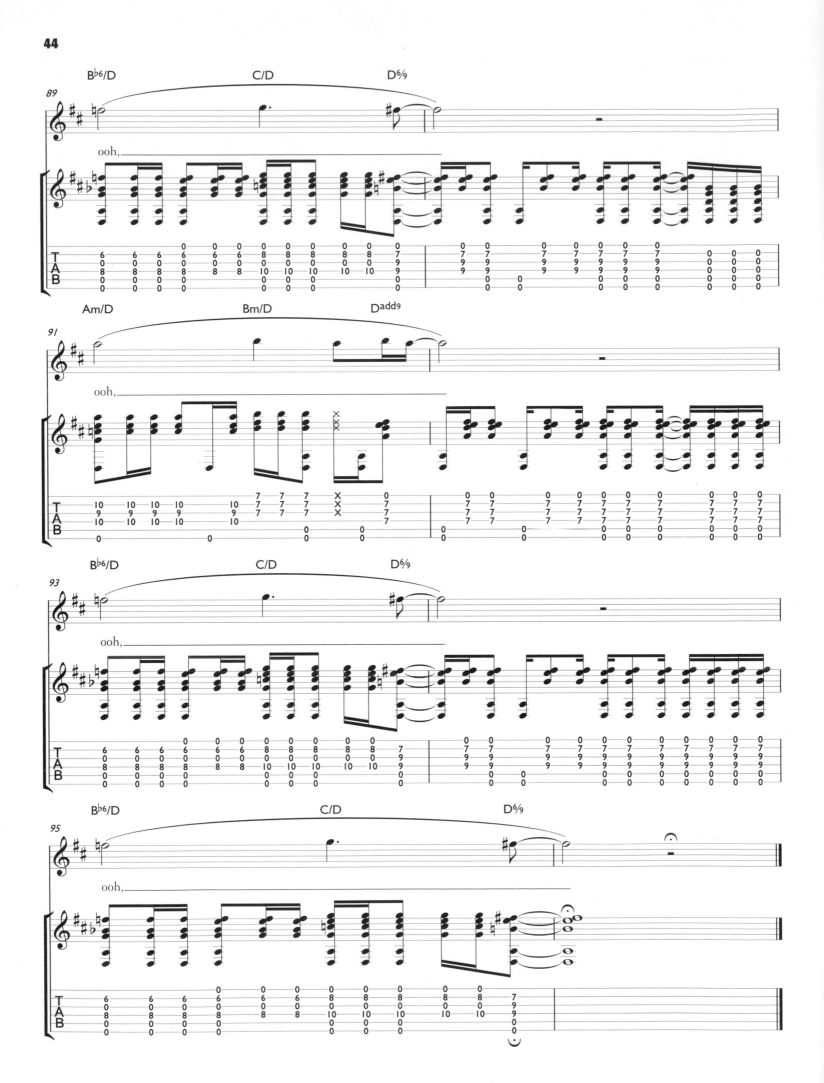

PARANOID ANDROID

Words and Music by
THOMAS YORKE, JONATHAN GREENWOOD,
COLIN GREENWOOD, EDWARD O'BRIEN and PHILIP SELWAY

Paranoid Android - 7 - 1

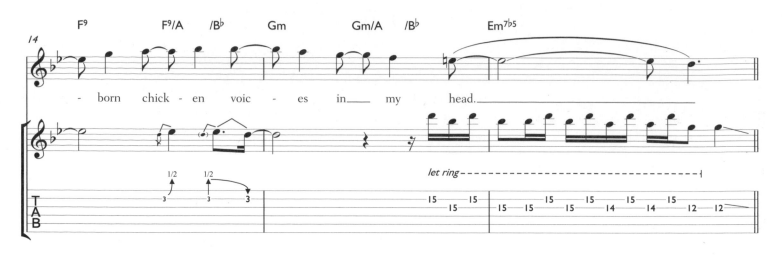

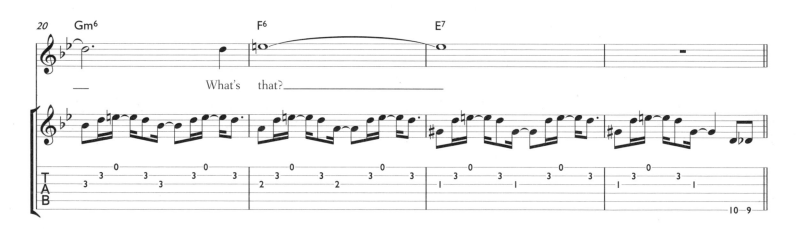

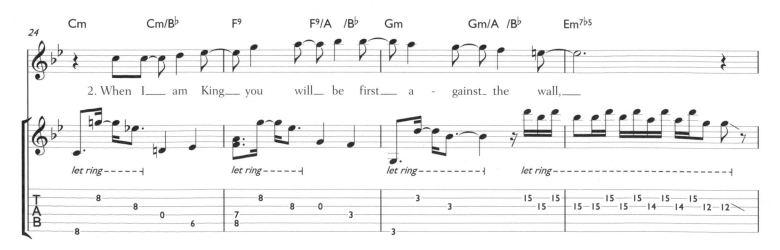

Paranoid Android - 7 - 2

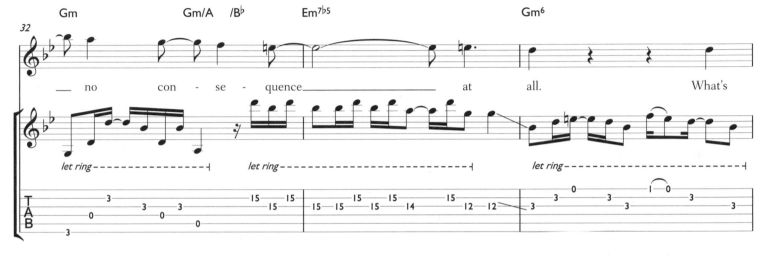

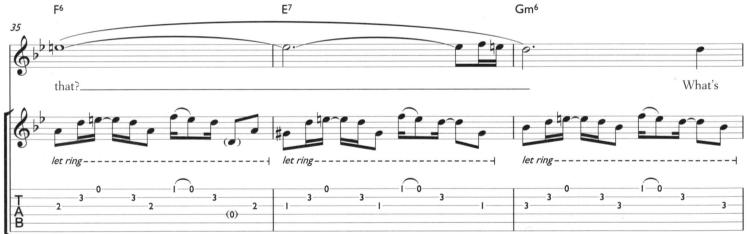

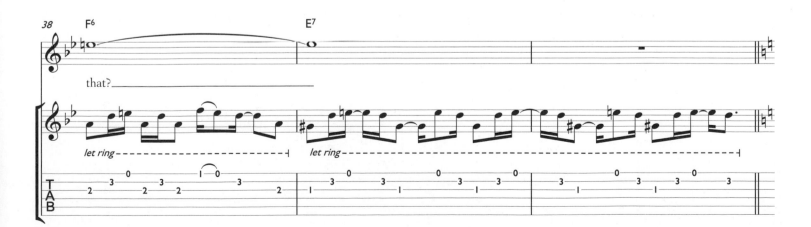

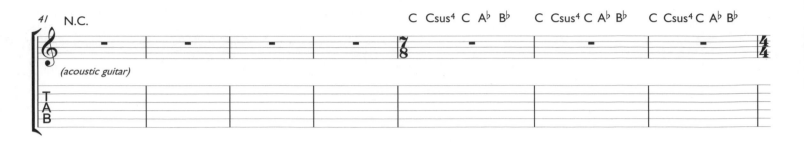

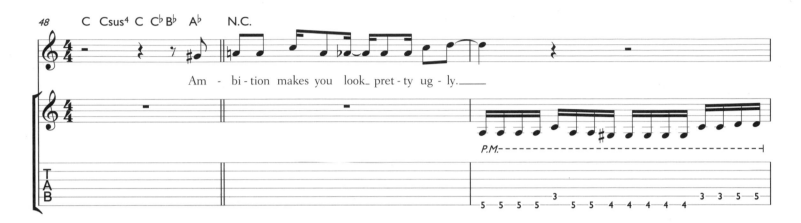

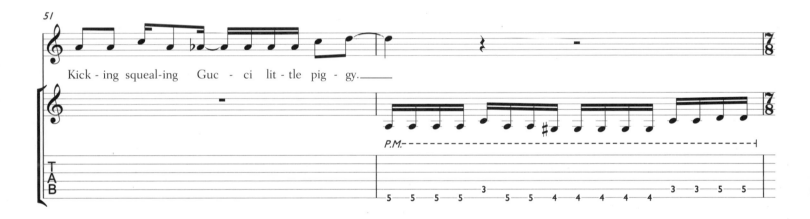

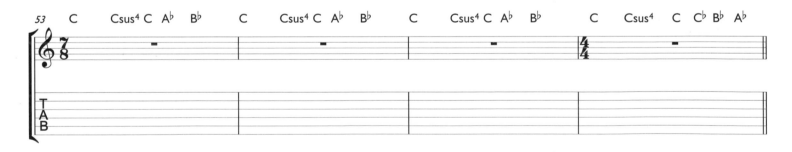

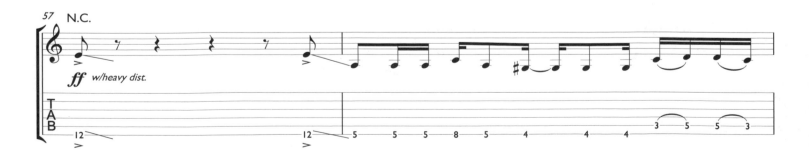

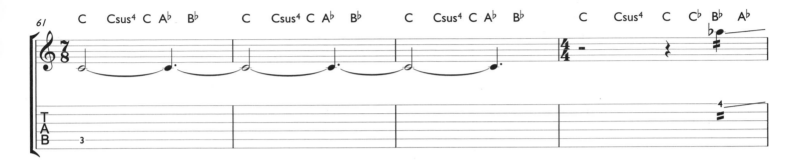

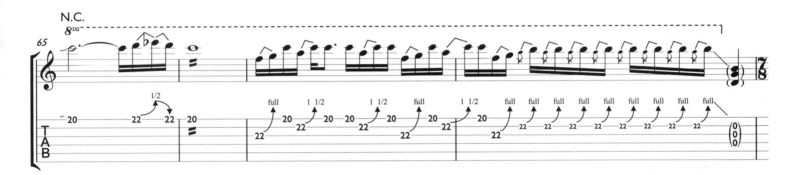

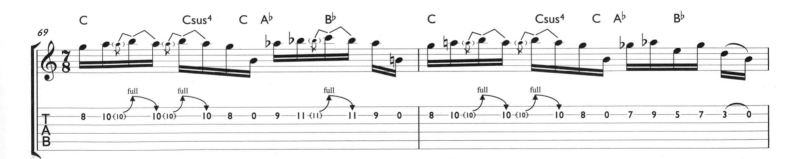

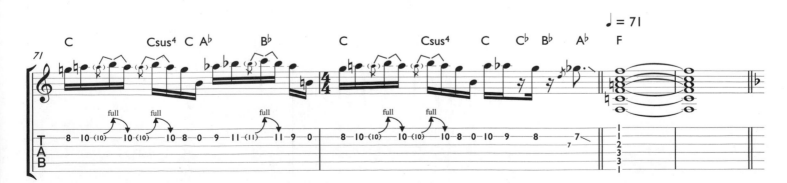

Paranoid Android - 7 - 5

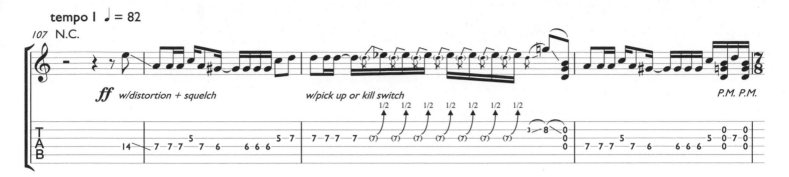

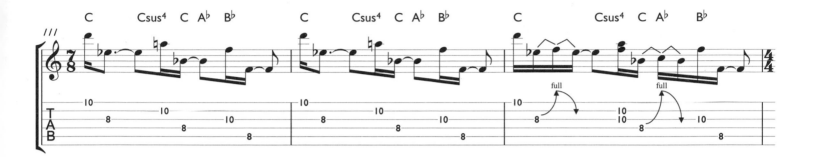

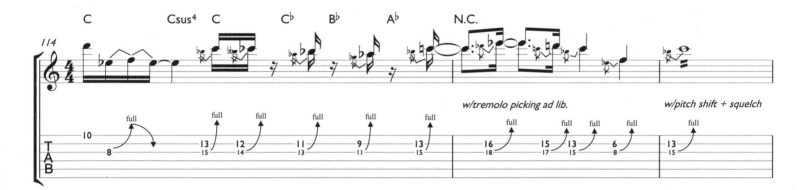

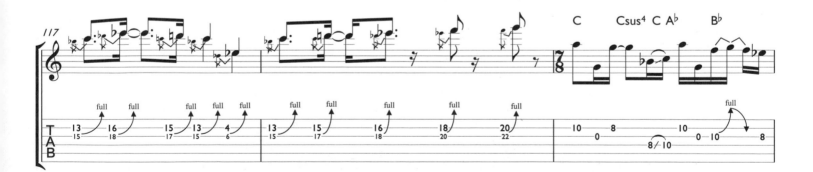

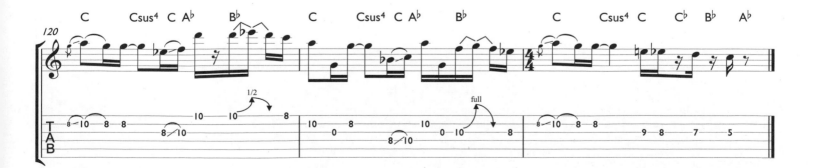

WEIRD FISHES/ARPEGGI

Words and Music by
THOMAS YORKE, JONATHAN GREENWOOD,
COLIN GREENWOOD, EDWARD O'BRIEN and PHILIP SELWAY

Weird Fishes/Arpeggi - 10 - 1

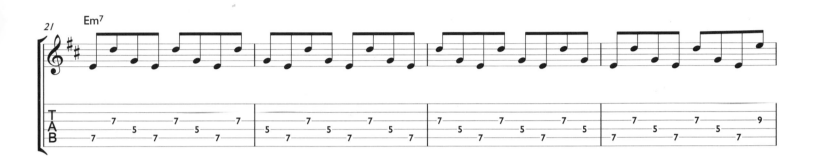

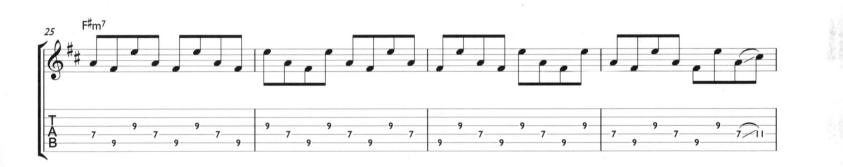

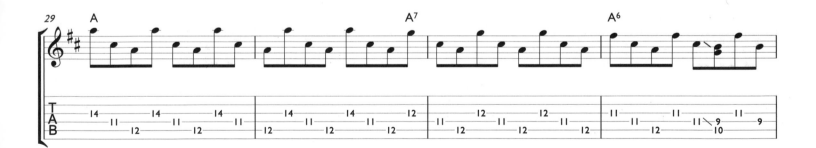

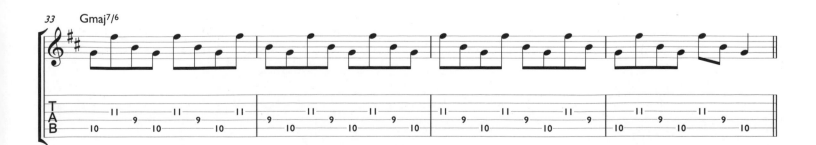

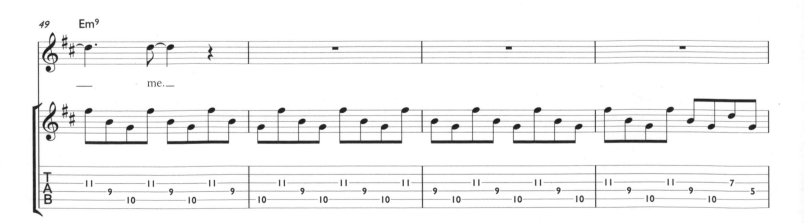

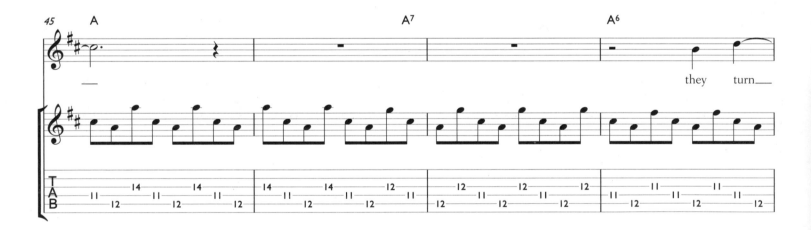

Weird Fishes/Arpeggi - 10 - 3

Why should I___ stay_____ here?

Why should I_____ stay?

2. I'd be cra -

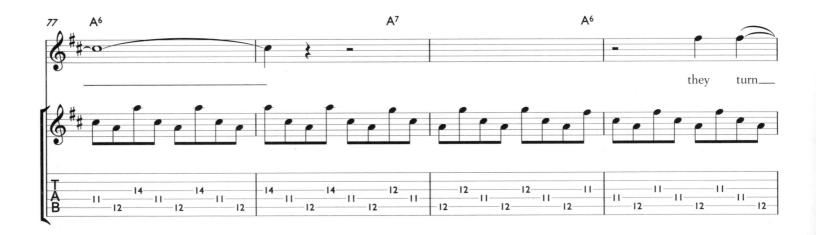

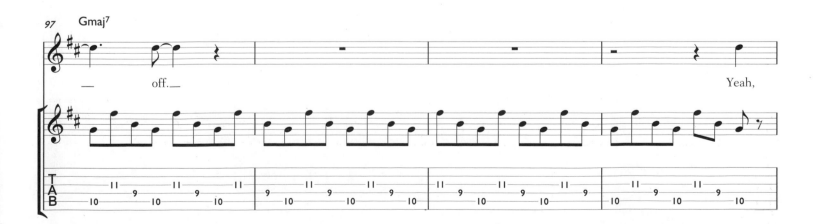

ev -'ry - bo - dy leaves___

if they get___ the chance,_____ and this___

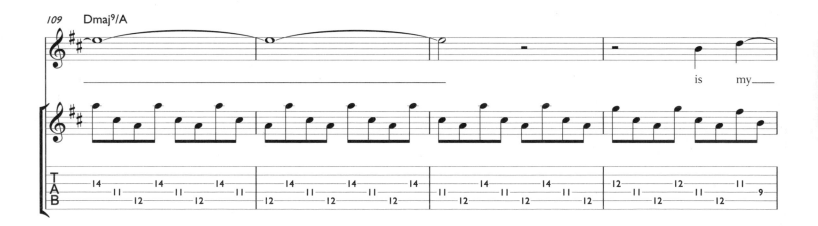

_____ is my___

___ chance.___ I get eat-

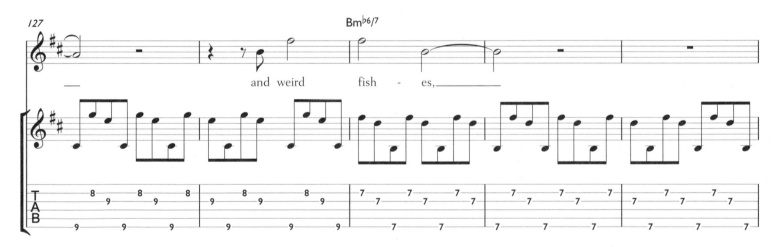

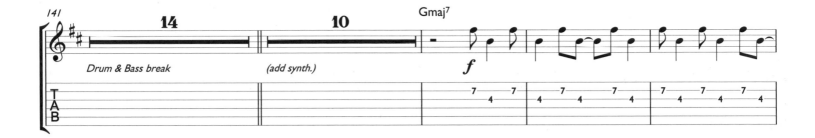

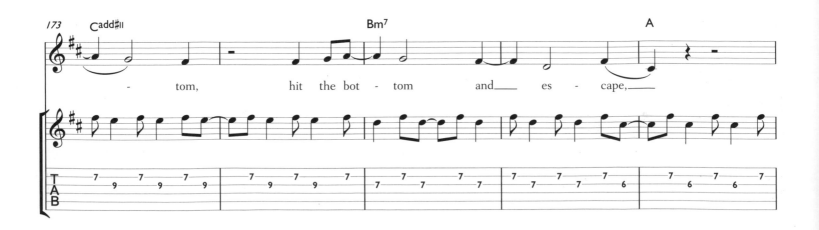

Guitar TAB Guide

Understanding Chord Boxes
Chord boxes show the neck of your guitar as if viewed head on—the vertical lines represent the strings (low E to high E, from left to right), and the horizontal lines represent the frets.

An X above a string means "don't play this string."

An O above a string means "play this open string."

The black dots show you where to put your fingers.

A curved line joining two dots on the fretboard represents a "barre." This means that you flatten one of your fingers (usually the first) so that you hold down all the strings between the two dots at the fret marked.

A fret marking at the side of the chord box shows you where chords that are played higher up the neck are located.

Tuning Your Guitar
The best way to tune your guitar is to use an electronic tuner. Alternatively, you can use relative tuning; this will ensure that your guitar is in tune with itself but won't guarantee that you will be in tune with the original track (or other musicians).

How to Use Relative Tuning
Fret the low E string at the 5th fret and pick the note; compare this with the sound of the open A string. The two notes should be in tune. If not, adjust the tuning of the A string until the two notes match.

Repeat this process for the other strings according to the diagram on the right:

Note that the B string should match the note at the 4th fret of the G string, whereas all the other strings match the note at the 5th fret of the string below.

As a final check, ensure that the bottom E string and top E string are in tune with each other.

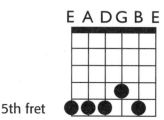

Detuning and Capo Use
If the song uses an unconventional tuning, it will say so clearly at the top of the music (for example, "6 = D" [tune the sixth string to D]) or "tune down a whole step." If a capo is used, it will tell you the fret number to which it must be attached. The standard notation will always be in the key at which the song sounds, but the guitar TAB will take tuning changes into account. Just detune/add the capo and follow the fret numbers. The chord symbols will show the sounding chord above and the chord you actually play below in brackets.

Use of Figures
Figures that occur several times in a song will be numbered (e.g., "Fig. 1," "Fig. 2," etc.) A dotted line underneath shows the extent of the "figure." When a phrase is to be played, it will be marked clearly in the score, along with the instrument that should play it.

Reading Guitar Tablature (TAB)
Guitar tablature, or TAB, illustrates the six strings of the guitar graphically, showing you where to put your fingers for each note or chord. TAB is usually shown with standard musical notation above it. The guitar TAB staff has six lines, each of them representing a different string. The top line is the high E string, the second line is the B string, and so on. Instead of using note heads, TAB uses numbers which show the fret number to be played by the left hand. The rhythm is indicated underneath the TAB staff. Ex. 1 (below) shows four examples of single notes.

Ex. 2 shows four different chords. The 3rd one (Asus4) should be played as a barre chord at the 5th fret. For the 4th chord (C9), you have to mute the string marked with an "x" (the A string, in this case) with a finger of your fretting hand in order to obtain the correct voicing.

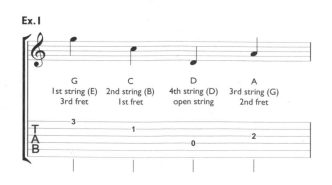

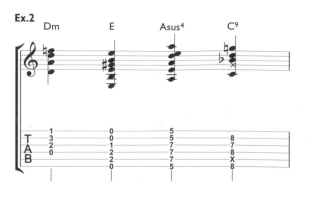

Picking Hand Techniques

1. Down and Up Strokes
These symbols [⊓ᴠ] show that some notes are to be played with a down stroke of the pick and others with up strokes.

2. Palm Mute
"P.M." indicates that you need to mute the notes with the palm of the picking hand by lightly touching the strings near the bridge.

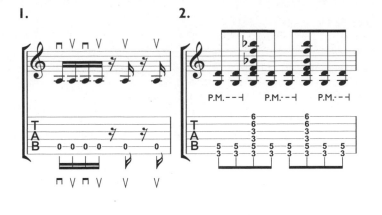

Fretting Hand Techniques

1. Hammer-on and Pull-off
These consist of two or more notes linked together by a slur. For hammer-ons, fret and play the lower note, then "hammer on" to the higher note with another finger. For a pull-off, play the higher note, then "pull off" to a lower note fretted with another finger. In both cases, only pick the first note.

2. Glissandi (Slides)
Fret and pick the first note, then slide the finger up to the second note. If they are slurred together, do not re-pick the second note.

3. Slow Glissando
Play the note(s) and slowly slide the finger(s) in the direction of the diagonal line(s).

4. Quick Glissando
Play the note(s) and immediately slide the finger(s) in the direction of the diagonal line(s).

5. Trills
Play the note and rapidly alternate between this note and the nearest one above in the key. If a note in brackets is shown before, begin with this note.

6. Fret-Hand Muting
Mute the notes with "X" with the fretting hand.

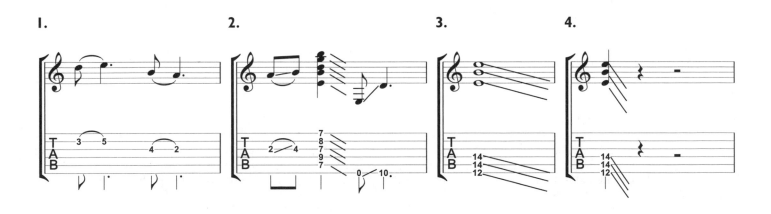

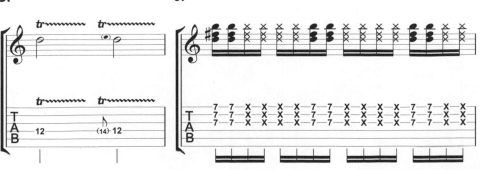

Bends and Vibrato

Bends

Bends are shown by the curved arrow pointing to a number (in the TAB).
Fret the first note and then bend the string up by the value of steps shown.

1. Half-Step Bend
The smallest conventional interval; equivalent to raising the note by one fret.

2. Whole-Step Bend
Equivalent to two frets.

3. Whole-Step-and-a-Half Bend
Equivalent to three frets.

4. Quarter-Step Bend
Bend by a slight degree, roughly equivalent to half a fret.

5. Bend and Release
Fret and pick the first note. Bend up for the length of the note shown. Follow with a release of the bend—letting the string fall back down to the original pitch.

6. Ghost Bend (Pre Bend)
Fret the bracketed note and bend quickly before picking the note.

7. Reverse Bend
Fret the bracketed note and bend quickly before picking the note, immediately let it fall back to the original.

8. Multiple Bends
A series of bends and releases joined together. Only pick the first note.

9. Unison Bend
Strike two indicated notes simultaneously and immediately bend the lower string up to the same pitch as the higher one.

10. Double-Note Bend
Play both notes and bend simultaneously by the value shown.

11. Bend Involving More Than One Note
Bend first note and hold the bend while striking a note on another string,

12. Bend Involving Stationary Notes
Play notes and bend lower string. Hold until release is indicated.

13. Vibrato
Shown by a wavy line. The fretting hand creates a vibrato effect using small, rapid up-and-down bends.

14. Bend and Tap Technique
Play and bend notes as shown, then sound the final pitch by tapping onto note as indicated (by + symbol).

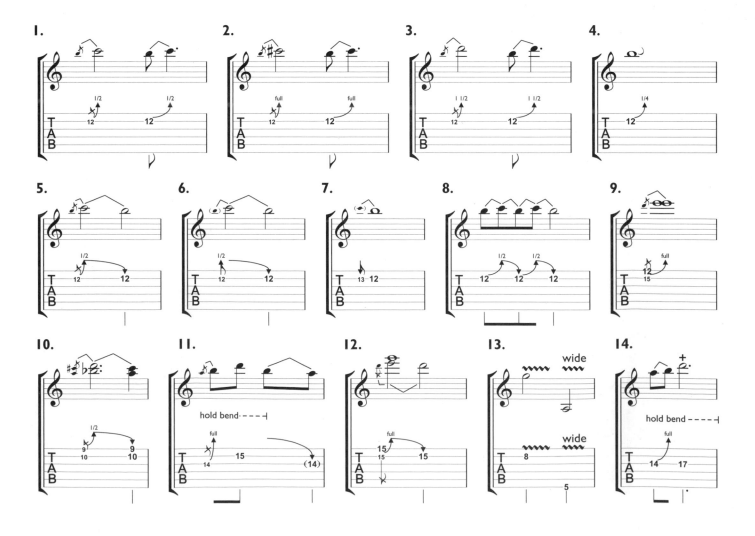